NEW IDEAS for
TODAY'S KNITTING

by Jean Leinhauser and Rita Weiss

STERLING

New York / London
www.sterlingpublishing.com

STERLING and the distinctive Sterling logo are registered trademarks of Sterling Publishing Co., Inc.

Library of Congress Cataloging-in-Publication Data

Leinhauser, Jean.
  New ideas for today's knitting / Jean Leinhauser and Rita Weiss.
    p. cm.
  Includes index.
  ISBN-13: 978-1-4027-2307-0
  ISBN-10: 1-4027-2307-5
  1. Knitting–Patterns. I. Weiss, Rita. II. Title.

TT820.L4563 2008
746.43'2041--dc22

                        2007020494

10 9 8 7 6 5 4 3 2 1

Published by Sterling Publishing Co., Inc.
387 Park Avenue South, New York, NY 10016
© 2008 by The Creative Partners™ LLC
Distributed in Canada by Sterling Publishing
c/o Canadian Manda Group, 165 Dufferin Street,
Toronto, Ontario, Canada M6K 3H6
Distributed in the United Kingdom by GMC Distribution Services
Castle Place, 166 High Street, Lewes, East Sussex, England
BN7 1XU
Distributed in Australia by Capricorn Link (Australia) Pty. Ltd.
P.O. Box 704, Windsor, NSW 2756, Australia

Printed in China
All rights reserved

Sterling ISBN-13: 978-1-4027-2307-0
        ISBN-10: 1-4027-2307-5

For information about custom editions, special sales, premium and corporate purchases, please contact Sterling Special Sales Department at 800-805-5489 or specialsales@sterlingpub.com.

Technical Editor: Ellen W. Liberles

Photography: James Jaeger
  Marshall Williams

Fashion Stylist: Christy Stevenson

Book Design: Graphic Solutions, inc-chgo

Produced by: The Creative Partners, LLC™

The authors thank the following contributing designers:

Dawn Adcock, Cary, Illinois

Angela Best, Toronto, Ontario, Canada

Rebecca Hatcher, Andover, Massachusetts

Margaret Hubert, Pawling, New York

Marnie MacLean, Playa Del Rey, California

Jordana Paige, Carmel, California

Myra Wood, Sherman Oaks, California

The authors extend their thanks and appreciation to the design departments at Cascade Yarns, S.R. Kertzer Ltd and Lion Brand Yarn for sharing many of their most creative designs with us.

Whenever we have used a special yarn we have given the brand name. If you are unable to find these yarns locally, write to the following manufacturers who will be able to tell you where to purchase their products, or consult their internet sites. We also wish to thank these companies for supplying yarn for this book.

Bernat Yarns
320 Livingston Avenue South
Listowel, Ontario
Canada N4W 3H3
www.bernat.com

Cascade Yarns
1224 Andover Park E
Tukwila, WA 98188
www.cascadeyarns.com

Classic Elite Yarns, Inc.
122 Western Avenue
Lowell, Massachusetts 01851
www.classiceliteyarns.com

S. R. Kertzer Limited
50 Trowers Rd
Woodbridge Ontario L4L 7K6
Canada
www.kertzer.com

Lion Brand Yarn
135 Kero Rd
Carlstadt, New Jersey 07072
www.lionbrand.com

Patons Yarns
2700 Dufferin Street
Toronto, Ontario
Canada M6B 4J3
www.patonsyarns.com

Plymouth Yarn Co., Inc.
500 Lafayette Street
P.O. Box 28
Bristol, Pennsylvania 19007-0028
www.plymouthyarn.com

TLC Yarns
Coats and Clark
Consumer Services
P. O. Box 12229
Greenville, South Carolina 29612-0229
www.coatsandclark.com

INTRODUCTION

What does today's knitter want?

Today's knitter is looking for glamorous – even daring – projects, and that's what we asked our designers to create for us. These edgy designs use the same knit and purl stitches we've always used, but oh what a different look these designers have achieved!

Innovation is the theme of this book, and our designers took today's beautiful new yarns, added their own touches and created fashions with a fresh and exciting new look.

Here you'll find the latest in "barely there" dresses to be worn only by the most daring, a furry coat, sexy lingerie, even bikinis – and many more designs sure to create a sensation.

Forget any pre-conceived ideas about knitting, and plunge right in to create the exciting look of here and now knitting. Just grab your needles and become part of the "wow!" look of knitting today.

Jean Leinhauser

Rita Weiss

CONTENTS

MELLOW YELLOW FAUX FUR COAT

Designed by Margaret Hubert

You'll sing a sweet fashion song in this canary-colored coat that will cause a sensation wherever it is worn. With deep cuffs and a shawl color, it is easy to wear and will become a favorite in your wardrobe.

MELLOW YELLOW FAUX FUR COAT

SIZES	Small	Medium	Large
Body Bust Measurements	38"- 40"	40"- 42"	44"- 46"
Finished Bust Measurements	47"	49"	52"

Note: Instructions are written for size Small; changes for sizes Medium and Large are in parentheses.

Materials

Bulky weight faux fur yarn
   1,000 (1,000, 1,100) g yellow
Note: Photographed model made with Friends Mustachio Banana
Size 8 (5mm) knitting needles
   (or size required for gauge)

Gauge

17 sts = 4" in garter stitch
   (knit every row)

INSTRUCTIONS

Note: Entire garment is worked in garter st.

BACK

Starting at bottom, CO 100 (106, 112) sts.

Knit until piece measures 10" (10 1/2", 11"). Dec 1 st each side on next row. Work even for 10" more. Dec 1 st each side on next row: 96 (102, 108) sts. Knit until piece measures 23 1/2" (24", 24 1/2") from CO row.

SHAPE ARMHOLE

BO 5 (6, 7) sts at beg of next 2 rows for underarm. Then dec one st each side every other row 5 times: 76 (80, 84) sts. Work even until armhole measures 10" (10 1/2", 11").

MELLOW YELLOW FAUX FUR COAT

SHOULDERS

BO 10 (11, 12) sts at beg of next 4 rows. BO rem 36 sts.

RIGHT FRONT

Starting at bottom CO 54 (57, 60) sts.

Knit until piece measures 10" (10 1/2", 11").

Decrease Row (mark beg this row for center front edge): Knit to last 2 sts, K2tog. Work even for 10" more.

Rep Decrease Row once more: 47 (49, 51) sts.

Work even until piece measures 23 1/2" (24", 24 1/2") from cast-on row.

Ending by working a right-side row.

SHAPE ARMHOLE

BO 5 (6, 7) sts for underarm, knit across. Then dec one st at beg of every wrong-side row 5 times: 37 (38, 39) sts. Work even until armhole measures 10" (10 1/2", 11").

SHAPE SHOULDER

BO 10 (11, 12) sts at beg of next 2 rows.

SHAWL COLLAR

Continue working on rem 27 sts for shawl collar until collar measures slightly longer than to center back of neck. BO loosely.

LEFT FRONT

Work as for Right Front, reversing shaping.

SLEEVE (make 2)

CO 68 (68, 70) sts. Knit even for 8" (this forms deep cuff). Then inc one st at each side, and rep the inc every 2", five times more: 80 (80, 82) sts. Work even until sleeve measures 21" (21 1/2", 22") from beg, or desired length. BO 5 (6, 7) sts at beg of next 2 rows for underarm, then dec one st at each side every other row till 26 sts rem. Work 0 (2, 4) more rows. BO.

FINISHING

Sew shoulder seams. Sew ends of collar tog at back. Center collar seam to center back of neck and sew in place. Center sleeve cap to shoulder seam, pin in place and sew. Sew underarm seams, being sure to sew on wrong side when sewing cuff turn-back.

WEAR IF YOU DARE

Designed by Angela Best

That little black dress updated with pizzazz and plenty of fringe. You'll turn heads whenever you appear in it.

WEAR IF YOU DARE

SIZES	Small	Medium	Large
Body Bust Measurements	32"	34"	38"
Finished Bust Measurements	32"	34"	38"

Note: Instructions are written for size Small; changes for sizes Medium and Large are in parentheses. Garment is stretchy; hip is 2" larger than bust.

Materials

Worsted weight chenille yarn with long eyelash
  component,
  300 (350, 350) g charcoal
Ribbon ladder yarn
  3 1/2 (3 1/2 , 5 1/2) oz black
*Note: Photographed model made with SR Kertzer
  Mexicali Lash chenille #3006 Charcoal and Estelle
  Designs ribbon ladder Dazzle #306*
String of silver pebble beads for back trim (optional),
  18" (20", 22")
6 stitch markers
Size J (6mm) crochet hook (for trim and ties)
1/2 yd contrast waste yarn cut into 3" lengths
29" Size 10 (6mm) circular knitting needle
  (or size required for gauge)

Gauge

14 sts and 16 rows = 4" in stock st (knit 1 row,
  purl 1 row)

Stitch Guide

Decrease (dec): K2 tog or P2tog

INSTRUCTIONS

SKIRT

Note: Skirt is worked in one piece in rnds to back opening.

Starting at bottom with chenille yarn, CO 120 (132, 144) sts; join, being careful not to twist rnds; place marker to indicate beg of rnds.

Work even in stock st (knit 1 row, purl 1 row) until piece measures 6" (7", 7 1/2").

Begin Skirt Shaping

Rnd 1: K1, place marker; K58 (64, 70), place marker, K2, place marker, K58 (64, 70), place marker, K1.

Rnd 2 (decrease rnd): K1, sl marker, dec, knit to 2 sts before marker, dec, sl marker, K2, sl marker, dec; knit to last 2 sts before marker, dec, sl marker, K1: 116 (128, 140).

Rnds 3 through 7: Work even.

Rnd 8: Rep Row 2: 112 (124, 136) sts.

Rep Rnds 3 through 8 two times more: 104 (116, 128) sts. Work 2 rows even.

Back Opening

Row 1 (right side): K22 (25, 28) sts; BO next 8 sts, knit back around to BO sts, turn: 96 (108, 120) sts. You will now work in rows.

Row 2: BO 5 sts, purl to 2 sts before marker, dec, P2, dec; purl front sts to 2 sts before marker, dec, P2, dec; purl to end of row: 87 (99, 111) sts.

Row 3: BO 5 sts, knit across: 82 (94, 106) sts.

Row 4: BO 4 sts, purl across: 78 (90, 102) sts.

Row 5: BO 4 sts, knit across: 74 (86, 98) sts.

Row 6: BO 4 sts, purl across: 70 (82, 94) sts.

Row 7: BO 4 sts; knit to 2 sts before marker, dec, K2, dec, work front to 2 sts before marker, dec, K2, dec; knit across: 62 (74, 86) sts. Remove markers.

Row 8: BO 2 sts, purl across: 60 (72, 84) sts.

Row 9: BO 2 sts, knit across: 58 (70, 82) sts.

Row 10: BO 2 sts, purl across: 56 (68, 80) sts.

Row 11: BO 2 sts, knit across: 54 (66, 78) sts.

Row 12: Purl across. Tie waste yarn in last st at armhole edge.

FRONT

Note: Continue to work in stock st (knit 1 row, purl 1 row).

Row 1: K1, dec, work to last 3 sts, dec, K1: 52 (64, 76) sts.

Rows 2 and 3: Work even.

Row 4: Purl 25 (31, 37) sts, BO 2 sts, purl 25 (31, 37) sts.

15

SOFTLY SCALLOPED NIGHTIE

Designed by Dawn Adcock

This little wisp of a gown is worked in the elegant Feather and Fan pattern, and accented with rows of feathery faux fur yarn. The drawstring waist adjustment lets it fit a wide range of sizes. It's sweetly feminine in white, or for the devil in you, make it in black or red.

SOFTLY SCALLOPED NIGHTIE

SIZES	Medium	Large
Body Bust Measurements	30"- 48"	48"- 60"
Finished Bust Measurements	42"	53"

Note: *Instructions are written for size Medium; changes for Large are in parentheses.*

Materials

Worsted weight yarn
  7 1/2 (10) oz white
Eyelash yarn
  3 1/2 (5 1/4) oz white
Note: *Photographed model made with Lion Brand® Wool-Ease® #501 White Frost and Bernat® Boa #81005 Dove*
Stitch marker
4 small safety pins
Size J (6mm) crochet hook
36" Size 13 (10mm) circular knitting needle
  (or size required for gauge)

Gauges

10 sts and 12 rows = 4" with worsted weight yarn
  in circular stock st (knit each row)
9 sts and 12 rows = 4" with eyelash yarn in circular
  stock st (knit each row)

Pattern Stitch

Feather and Fan Pattern

Multiple of 18 sts

Rnd 1: *(K2tog) 3 times, (YO, K1) 6 times, (K2tog) 3 times; rep from * around.

Rnds 2 through 6: Knit.

Repeat Rows 1 through 6 for pattern.

INSTRUCTIONS

Starting at bottom of skirt with one strand of each yarn held tog, loosely CO 144 (180) sts.

EDGING:

Working flat for first row, purl one row with both yarns held tog.

At end of row, cut eyelash yarn. Join into round with purl side facing out, being careful not to twist stitches when joining. Place a marker on right-hand needle to indicate beg of rnd.

SKIRT (worked with worsted weight yarn only)
Foundation Rnd: Knit.

Repeat Feather and Fan pattern 7 times.

Skirt should now measure about 16" to 17" to bottom of rounded scallop point.

Note: *To lengthen skirt (which will require more yarn), rep Rnds 1 through 6 for desired length, ending by working a Rnd 6.*

Eyelet Rnd (for center tie): *K2tog, YO, K2; rep from * around. Knit 1 rnd. Cut worsted weight yarn.

TOP (worked with eyelash yarn only)
Join eyelash yarn.

Decrease Rnd: *K1, K2tog; rep from * around: 96 (120) sts. Knit even for 6" (18 rnds), or desired length of top. Cut eyelash yarn, join worsted weight yarn.

Note: *Top will stretch lengthwise when worn after attaching ties, and will also draw in widthwise as it hangs from the shoulder.*

SOFTLY SCALLOPED NIGHTIE

TOP EDGING

With worsted weight yarn, knit one rnd. Then BO very loosely as to knit; loose BO allows top edge to stretch to form points after ties are attached.

FINISHING:

Shoulder Ties

Mark tie placement, two on front and two on back, with safety pins. Mark each of the following sets of sts on BO edge as follows, counting from first st bound off:

Sts 12 and 13 (15 and 16)

Sts 36 and 37 (45 and 46)

Sts 60 and 61 (75 and 76)

Sts 84 and 85 (105 and 106)

With crochet hook, join eyelash yarn with a sl st between the first set of marked sts, sc in same place. Ch for 14" (16"), or desired strap length. Finish off; weave in ends.

Work 3 more ties in same manner between other marked sets of sts.

Waist Tie

With worsted weight yarn and crochet hook, make a chain 60" (100") long. Finish off, weave in ends. Thread chain through eyelet rnd at waist, starting and ending at front center of skirt. Tie in bow at front.

Using yarn tail at CO edge of skirt, sew gap of first straight purl row closed on side.

Tie shoulder ties at desired length. Pull on CO row at bottom to stretch it and allow scallops to ruffle.

HERE COMES THE BRIDE

Designed by Rita Weiss

Not for your average bride, this is the dress for the non-conventional one (or the second time around). Wear the capelet during the ceremony, remove it when it's time to party.

HERE COMES THE BRIDE

SIZES	Small	Medium	Large
Body Bust Measurements	32"	34"	36"
Finished Bust Measurements	29 1/2"	33 1/2"	37 1/2"

Note: Instructions are written for size Small; changes for sizes Medium and Large are in parentheses.

Materials

Metallic Worsted weight stretchy yarn
15 3/4 (17 1/2, 19 1/4) oz silver

Note: A stretchy yarn is essential for the fit of this garment. Photographed model made with Lion Brand® Glitterspun #150 Silver

Stitch marker

Size 9 (5.5mm) knitting needles (or size required for gauge)

16" and 26" Size 9 (5.5mm) circular knitting needle

Two Size 9 (5.5mm) double point needles

Gauge

16 sts = 4" in stock stitch (knit 1 row, purl 1 row)

Stitch Guide

Slip, slip, knit (SSK): Slip next two stitches as if to knit, one at a time to right-hand needle, Insert tip of left-hand needle into fronts of these stitches from left to right. Knit them together. One stitch has been decreased.

DRESS

INSTRUCTIONS

BACK

With straight needles, starting at bottom edge, CO 75 (83, 91) sts.

EDGING

Row 1: Knit.

Row 2: Knit.

LACE BORDER

Row 1 (right side): K2; *YO, K2, K3tog, K2, YO, K1; rep from * across to last st, K1.

Row 2 and all even rows (wrong side): K1, purl to last st, K1.

Rows 3, 5, 7: Rep Row 1.

Row 9: K1, K2tog; *K2, YO, K1, YO, K2, K3tog; rep from * across, ending last rep with K2, YO, K1, YO, K2, SSK, K1.

Rows 11, 13, 15: Rep Row 9.

Row 16: Rep Row 2.

Rep Rows 1 through 16 until piece measures 12" from CO row, ending by working a wrong-side row. This completes the lace pattern.

Decrease Rows:

Row 1 (right side): K1, K2 tog, knit to last 3 sts, SSK, K1: 73 (81, 89) sts.

Row 2: K1, purl to last st, K1.

Rep Rows 1 and 2 until 59 (67, 75) sts rem, ending by working a wrong-side row.

Work even in stock st (knit 1 row, purl 1 row) until piece measures 26" from CO edge, ending by working a right side (knit) row.

Knit 6 rows. BO.

FRONT

Work same as back.

STRAPS

Following directions for making I-Cord on page 126, CO 3 sts and work 2 pieces of I-Cord, each approximately 18" long.

FINISHING

Block pieces if necessary. Sew side seams. Sew I-Cord straps to front and back approximately 3" in from each side seam.

CAPELET

INSTRUCTIONS

Starting at bottom with circular needle, CO 192 sts. Join, being careful not to twist sts; place marker to indicate start of rnd.

EDGING

Rnds 1 through 4: Purl.

LACE BODY

Rnd 1 (right side): *K1, YO, K2, K3tog, K2, YO; rep from * to end of rnd.

Rnd 2 and all even rnds (wrong side): Knit.

Rnds 3, 5, 7: Rep Rnd 1

Rnd 9: K2tog; *K2, YO, K1, YO, K2, K3tog; rep from *, ending last rep with K2, YO, K1, YO, K1, SSK.

Rnds 11, 13, 15: Rep Row 9.

Rnd 16: Rep Rnd 2.

Rep Rnds 1 through 16 until piece measures 12" from CO edge, ending by working an odd-numbered rnd. This ends the lace section.

First Decrease Rnd: Knit around, evenly decreasing 64 sts: 128 sts.

Continue working in circular Stock St (knit every rnd) until piece measures 14 1/2" from CO edge.

Second Decrease Rnd: Working in circular Stock St, knit around, evenly decreasing 42 sts: 86 sts.

Work two rows of circular Stock St.

Third Decrease Rnd: Working in circular Stock St, knit around, evenly decreasing 30 sts: 56 sts.

Continue working in circular stock st until piece measures 16" from CO edge.

NECK SHAPING

Rnd 1: Purl.

Rnd 2: Knit.

BO loosely.

LITTLE BLACK DRESS

Designed by
Margaret Hubert

This little wisp of a dress has attitude! It's sure to turn heads wherever it goes.

LITTLE BLACK DRESS

SIZES	Small	Medium	Large
Body Bust Measurements	36"- 38"	38"- 40"	40"- 42"
Finished Bust Measurements	36"	38"	40"

Note: Instructions are written for size Small; changes for sizes Medium and Large are in parentheses.

Note: Garment is quite stretchy.

Materials

Worsted weight yarn
  21 (21, 22 3/4) oz black (A)
Bulky weight faux fur (B)
  7 (7, 8 3/4) oz black
*Note: Photographed model made with Lion Brand®
  Glitterspun #153 Onyx (A) and Lion Brand® Festive
  Fur #153 Onyx (B)*
4 stitch markers
2 large stitch holders
36" Size 6 (4mm) circular knitting needle
  (or size required for gauge)
16" Size 6 (4mm) circular knitting needle

Gauge

4 sts = 1" in stock st (knit 1 row, purl 1 row)

INSTRUCTIONS

Note: Dress is worked in one piece in the round from the neck down. Worsted weight yarn may be carried loosely over the faux fur stripes, but faux fur must be cut and re-attached each time.

Starting at neckline with longer needle and A, CO 96 (96, 96) sts; join, being careful not to twist.

Rnds 1 through 4: Knit.

Rnd 5 (turning ridge): K1; * YO, K2tog; rep from * around, end K1.

Rnds 6 through 9: Knit.

From now to hemline, work in striping pattern of 2 rounds B, 12 rounds A, as follows:

Rnd 1: K34, place marker on needle (back section); K14, place marker (first sleeve section); K34, place marker (front section); K14, place marker (2nd sleeve section and end of rnd); you may want to make last marker a different color to indicate end of rnd.

Rnd 2: Inc one st before and after each marker as follows: sl marker, K1, inc one st in the next st; * knit to within 2 sts of next marker, inc 1 in next st, K1, sl marker, K1, inc 1 in next st; rep from * 2 times more; knit to within 2 sts of last marker, inc 1 in next st, K1.

Rnd 3: Knit, sl markers as you come to them.

Rep Rnds 2 and 3, being sure to keep striping pattern, until front and back sections have 72 (76, 80) sts, and each sleeve section has 52 (56, 60) sts.

DIVIDE FOR BODY

Work even across back and one sleeve, place sleeve section just worked on a st holder; work across front and 2nd sleeve, place sleeve just worked on another st holder. Leave markers in place to denote underarms. Continue working back and front in rnds, in striping pattern as established, as follows:

Work 1 1/2" (2", 2 1/2") even on 144 (152, 160) sts , then dec one st before and after each underarm marker: 140 (148, 156) sts.

Continue in striping patt, dec one st at each side of each underarm marker every 2" two times more: 132 (140, 148) sts. Work even until 8" (8 1/2", 9") from underarm, then inc one st each side of each underarm marker, and rep the inc every 1" two times more: 144

(152, 160) sts. Work even until piece measures 22" (23", 24") from beg, ending by working a B stripe.

HEM (work with A)

Rnds 1 through 4: Knit.

Rnd 5 (turning ridge): K1; *YO, K2tog; rep from * around, end K1.

Rnds 6 through 9: Knit. At end of Rnd 9, BO loosely.

RIGIIT SLEEVE

Place 52 (56, 60) sts from holder onto shorter circular needle, CO 2 sts, knit around, CO 2 sts, join. Rep Rnds 1 through 9 of Hem. BO loosely.

LEFT SLEEVE

Work same as Right Sleeve.

FINISHING

Turn hemlines under at turning ridge at neck, skirt and sleeve edges and sew in place.

Sew underarm seams.

TEENY WEENY BIKINI

Designed by Marnie MacLean and Rita Weiss

Celebrate the warmth of summer with a knit bikini, perfect for a swim or just showing off on the shore.

BEACH COVER-UP

*Too much sun?
Wear this easy-to-make
top over your suit.
Finished swimming for
the day? Wear the top
over your jeans.*

BEACH COVER-UP

SIZES	Small	Medium	Large	X- Large
Body Bust Measurements	30"- 34"	36"- 40"	42"- 46"	48"- 52"
Finished Bust Measurements	36"	42"	48"	54"

Note: Instructions are written for size Small; changes for sizes Medium, Large and X-Large are in parentheses.

Materials

Worsted weight cotton/wool blend yarn
   14 (14, 17 1/2, 17 1/2) oz black
Note: Photographed model made with Cascade Yarns Sierra #2 Black
Stitch holder
Size G (4mm) crochet hook
Size 9 (5.5mm) knitting needles
   (or size required for gauge)

Gauge

16 sts = 4" in pattern
Yarn manufacturer's gauge note: The garment is knit loosely so when measuring gauge, pull down slightly since the garment will pull down when worn.

Stitch Guide

Pattern Stitch
Row 1: Knit.
Row 2: Knit.
Row 3: Purl.
Row 4: Knit.

Increase: Knit (or purl) in front and in back of same st.

Reverse sc (rev sc): Ch 1; *insert hook in next st to the right (instead of left) of hook and draw up a lp; YO and draw through both lps on hook; rep from *, working to the right instead of the left. This gives a corded edge: rev sc made.

INSTRUCTIONS

BACK

Starting at bottom, CO 11 sts.

Row 1 (wrong side): Knit, inc one st at end of row: 12 sts.

Row 2: Knit, inc one st at end of row: 13 sts.

Row 3: Purl, inc one st at end of row: 14 sts.

Row 4: Knit, inc one st at end of row: 15 sts.

Rep Rows 1 through 4 until there are 72 (84, 96, 108) sts.

Continue working in pattern until piece measures 21" from CO edge, ending by working a Row 4.

SHAPE ARMHOLES

Row 1: BO 3 (4, 5, 6) sts at beg of row; knit across: 69 (80, 91, 102) sts.

Row 2: Rep **Row 1:** 66 (76, 86, 96) sts.

Row 3: P2tog, purl to last 2 sts, P2tog: 64 (74, 84, 94) sts.

Row 4: K2tog, knit to last 2 sts, K2tog: 62 (72, 82, 92) sts.

Row 5: K26 (30, 35, 39) for shoulder, BO 10 (12, 12, 14) sts for neck, K26 (30, 35, 39) for other shoulder.

Row 6: K26 (30, 35, 39). Place rem 26 (30, 35, 39) sts on st holder for other shoulder.

Row 7: P2tog, purl across.

Rows 8, 9 and 10: K2tog, knit across: 22 (26, 31, 35) sts at end of Row 10.

Row 11: P2tog, purl across.

Row 12, 13 and 14: K2tog, knit across: 18 (22, 27, 31) sts at end of Row 14.

Row 15: P2tog, purl across: 17 (21, 26, 30) sts.

For Size Small Only

Row 16: Knit.

Work even in patt until armhole measures 8 1/2". BO all sts.

For Size Medium Only

Row 16: K2tog, knit across: 20 sts.

Row 17: Knit.

Work even in patt until armhole measures 8 1/2". BO all sts.

For Size Large Only

Row 16: K2tog, knit across: 25 sts.

Row 17: Knit.

Row 18: K2 tog, knit across: 24 sts.

Row 19: Purl.

Work even in patt until armhole measures 8 1/2". BO all sts.

For Size X-Large Only

Row 16: K2tog, knit across: 29 sts.

Row 17: Knit.

Row 18: K2tog, knit across: 28 sts.

Row 19: Purl.

BERIBBONED CAMISOLE

Designed by Margaret Hubert

Colorful swirls of ribbons form the straps for this party-perfect cami. The three bright ribbons spark the textured black of the knitted fabric.

BERIBBONED CAMISOLE

SIZES	Small	Medium	Large
Body Bust Measurements	34"	36"	38"
Finished Bust Measurements	32"	34"	36"

Note: Instructions are written for size Small; changes for sizes Medium and Large are in parentheses.

Materials

DK or sport weight yarn
   7 (7, 8 3/4) oz black
Note: Photographed model made with Patons® Grace #60040 Night
4 yd each of 3 different colors,
   3/8" wide grosgrain ribbon.
Size 5 (3.75mm) knitting needles
Size 6 (4mm) knitting needles
   (or size required for gauge)

Gauge

6 sts = 1" on larger needles in
   Pattern St

Stitch Guide

Pattern Stitch

Row 1 (wrong side): Knit.

Row 2: K1; *P1, K1; rep from * across.

INSTRUCTIONS

Note: Camisole rows are worked vertically between top and bottom.

BACK

With larger needles, CO 77 (79, 81) sts for right underarm edge. Work in Pattern Stitch for 4 1/2" (5", 5 1/4"), ending by working a right-side row.

FURRY FUN

What could be more fun than a bright red faux fur jacket!

FURRY FUN

SIZES	Small	Medium	Large	X-Large
Body Bust Measurements	34"	36"	38"	40"-42"
Finished Bust Measurements	37"	40"	42 1/2"	45 3/4"

Note: Instructions are written for size Small; changes for sizes Medium, Large and X-Large are in parentheses.

Materials

Faux fur type yarn
 19 1/4 (19 1/4, 21, 21) oz red
Sport weight yarn
 10 (10, 10, 15) oz red
Note: Photographed model made with Lion Brand® Fun Fur #113 Red and Lion Brand® Wool-Ease® Sportweight #102 Ranch Red
2 stitch holders
Size 11 (8mm) knitting needles (or size required for gauge)

Gauge

14 sts and 15 rows = 4" in stock st (knit 1 row, purl 1 row) with one stand of each yarn held tog

Stitch Guide

M1 (make 1): Make one st by picking up horizontal bar lying before next stitch and knitting into back of this bar: increase made.

INSTRUCTIONS

Note: Entire garment is worked with two strands (one strand of each yarn) held tog.

BACK

With 2 strands of yarn (one strand of each yarn held tog), CO 61 (66, 71, 76) sts.

Rows 1 and 2: Knit.

Row 3: Purl.

Row 4: Knit.

Row 5: Purl.

Work even in stock st until piece measures about 5 3/4" (6", 6 1/4", 6 1/2").

Increase Row: Inc 1 st at each end of row.

Work even in stock st for 5", then rep Increase Row once more: 65 (70, 75, 80) sts. Work even until piece measures 11 1/2" from cast-on row, ending by working a wrong-side row.

SHAPE ARMHOLES

BO 3 sts at beg of next 2 rows, then BO 2 sts at beg of next 2 rows. Dec one st at each end on next row, then every other row 3 (3, 3, 4) times more: 47 (52, 57, 60) sts. Work even until armhole measures 8" (8 1/2", 9", 9 1/2"), ending by working a wrong-side row.

SHAPE NECK AND SHOULDER

For Sizes Small, Medium and Large Only:

BO 7 (8, 9) sts at beg of next 4 rows, then BO rem 19 (20, 21) sts for back of neck.

For Size X-Large Only:

BO 9 sts at beg of next 2 rows, then BO 10 sts at beg of next 2 rows; BO rem 22 sts for back of neck.

LEFT FRONT

With 2 strands of yarn, CO 32 (36, 39, 42) sts.

Rows 1 and 2: Knit.

Row 3: Purl to last 4 sts, K4 (for center front band; mark this edge as center front).

Row 4: Knit.

Work even in stock st, working each purl row as Row 3, until piece measures 5" from beg. Then inc one st at side edge on next row. Work even for 5" more, then inc one st at side edge: 34 (38, 41, 44) sts.

Work even until piece measures 11 1/2" from beg, ending by working a wrong-side row.

SHAPE ARMHOLE

BO 3 sts at beg of next row for underarm, work one row even. BO 2 sts at beg of next row, work one row even. Dec one st at beg of next row, then every other row 3 (3, 3, 4) times more: 25 (29, 32, 34) sts.

Work even until armhole measures 6" (6 1/2", 7", 7 1/2"), ending by working a wrong-side row.

SHAPE NECK AND SHOULDER

Row 1: Knit to last 7 (9, 10, 11) sts, and place them on a holder for collar.

Row 2: P2tog, purl across.

Row 3: Knit.

Rep Rows 2 and 3, three times more. At the same time, when armhole measures same as back, decrease for shoulder, ending by working a wrong-side row.

SHOULDER DECREASES

For Sizes Small, Medium and Large Only:

Row 1: Starting at arm edge, BO 7 (8, 9) sts, knit across.

Row 2: Shaping neck edge, purl.

Row 3: BO 7 (8, 9) sts.

For Size X-Large Only:

At arm edge, BO 9 sts once, then BO 10 sts once, completing neck shaping at front edge.

RIGHT FRONT

Work same as Left Front, reversing shaping.

SLEEVE (make 2)

With 2 strands of yarn held tog, CO 26 (28, 30, 34) sts.

Rows 1 and 2: Knit.

Row 3: Purl.

Row 4: Knit.

Row 5: Purl.

Row 6 (increase row): K1, M1, knit to last st, M1, K1.

Continue in stock st, repeating increased row every 6th row 9 times more: 46 (48, 50, 54) sts.

Work even until piece measures 16 1/2" (17", 17", 17") from beg, or desired length to unerarm, ending by working a wrong-side row.

SHAPE SLEEVE CAP

BO 3 sts at beg of next 2 rows for underarm.

Decrease Row: Dec one st at each end of row. Rep dec every other row 8 times more. BO rem 24 (26, 28, 32) sts.

FINISHING

Sew shoulder seams.

Collar: With right side facing and 2 strands of yarn held tog, K7 (9, 10, 11) sts from right front holder, pick up and K32 (33, 34, 35) sts evenly around neck edge, K7 (9, 10, 11) sts from left front holder: 46 (51, 54, 57) sts. Knit 10 rows. BO tightly.

Sew sleeves into armholes; sew side and sleeve seams.

FANCY FEET AND FINGERS

Designed by Myra Wood

Dancing hands and dancing feet need to be dressed up also. Make this pair of toeless socks and fingerless gloves just for fun!

JUST FOR FUN TANK TOP

So simple to make; so easy to wear, this delightful garment will fit in everyone's wardrobe.

HOW INCREDIBLE!

Designed by Margaret Hubert

This is true elegance! A hint of metallic glitz and silky ribbons are combined in an interesting pattern stitch. The classic Chanel style is accented with a delicate black ruffle. This is a major piece for anyone's wardrobe!

SOPHISTICATED TANK

Designed by Jordana Paige

All eyes will turn to look at the glamorous gal wearing this striped beauty.

SOPHISTICATED TANK

SIZES	X-Small	Small	Medium	Large	X-Large
Body Bust Measurements	30"	32"	34"	36"	38"
Finished Bust Measurements	32"	34"	36"	38"	40"

Note: Instructions are written for size X-Small; changes for sizes Small, Medium, Large and X-Large are in parentheses.

Materials

Worsted weight yarn
   5 1/4 (5 1/4, 7, 7, 7) oz dark grey
      (MC)
   3 1/2 (3 1/2, 5 1/4, 5 1/4, 5 1/4) oz
      lime (A)
   3 1/2 (3 1/2, 5 1/4, 5 1/4, 5 1/4) oz
      pink (B)
Note: Photographed model made
   with Classic Elite Bam Boo
   #4948 Storm (MC), #4920
   Citrine (A) and #4954 Cherise (B)
Stitch holder
Size 7 (4.5mm) knitting needles
   (or size required for gauge)
Two Size 7 (4.5mm) double-point knitting needles

Gauge

20 sts and 24 rows = 4" in stock st
   (knit 1 row, purl 1 row)

Stitch Guide

SSK (sl, sl, knit): Sl next 2 sts one at a time to right needle, then knit these 2 sts tog.

M1: Make one st by picking up horizontal lp lying before next st and knitting into back of lp: increase made.

Stripe Pattern

All pieces are worked in Stripe Pattern as follows:
   *2 rows MC
   2 rows A
   2 rows B
Repeat from * for pattern.

INSTRUCTIONS

FRONT

Bra Section

With MC, CO 80 (85, 90, 95, 100) sts. Work in stock st in stripe pattern until piece measures 4 3/4" (5 1/2", 5 3/4", 6 1/4", 6 3/4"), ending by working a wrong-side row. With MC, knit 3 rows for top border. With wrong side facing, BO.

Body

Note: Body rows are worked vertically between top and bottom.

With MC, CO 52 sts.

Row 1: K48 sts; join a 2nd ball of MC and K4 for garter st hem border.

Row 2: K4, drop 2nd ball; pick up first ball of MC, purl to end of row.

Continue in stock st in stripe patt, maintaining a 4-st garter st border in MC. AT SAME TIME when work measures 3 1/2" (4", 4 1/2", 5", 5 1/2") with right side facing: K2, M1, work to end. Rep this inc every 4 rows 2 times, then every 2 rows 5 times.

Work even until piece measures 8" (8 1/2", 9", 9 1/2", 10"). With right side facing, K2, SSK, work to end. Rep this dec every 2 rows 4 times more, then every 4 rows 3 times. Continue in stripe pattern with garter st border until piece measures 16" (17", 18", 19", 20"). BO all sts.

SOPHISTICATED TANK

BACK

Note: Back is worked sideways.

Body

With MC, CO 86 (88, 91, 93, 96) sts.

Row 1: K82 (84, 87, 89, 92) sts, join a 2nd ball of MC and K4 for garter st hem border.

Row 2: K4, drop 2nd ball; pick up first ball of MC and purl to end.

Continue in stock st in stripe patt, maintaining the 4-st garter st border in MC.

When piece measures 16" (17", 18", 19", 20"), BO all sts.

Top

On top edge (opposite garter stitch hem border) measure and mark 2" in from both sides. With right side facing, and with MC pick up and K60 (66, 70, 76, 80) sts between markers. You will now work the top back section in stock st stripe pattern, maintaining 4 sts at beg and end of each row in MC garter st for border. You will need a ball of MC at each edge.

Row 1 (wrong side): K4 with MC, with appropriate stripe color P1, P2tog, purl to last 7 sts, P2tog, P1; K4 with MC.

Row 2: K4 with MC, with appropriate stripe color knit to last 4 sts, K4 with MC.

Rep these 2 rows 12 (13, 13, 14, 14) more times: 34 (38, 42, 46, 50) sts.

Right Back

With right side facing, work 17 (19, 21, 23, 25) sts for Right Back, place rem 17 (19, 21, 23, 25) sts on a st holder for Left Back.

Decrease Row 1: K4 with appropriate stripe color, purl to last 7 sts, P2tog tbl, P1, K4 with MC.

Decrease Row 2: Work one row even.

Rep these 2 rows 5 more times: 11 (13, 15, 17, 19) sts. Work even for 3/4". BO.

Left Back

Place sts from st holder onto needle. Work as for Right Back, reversing shaping.

I-Cord for Tie

With MC and double-point needles, CO 3 sts. Work I-cord (see page 126) until piece measures 78". BO.

FINISHING

Thread a length of MC into a tapestry needle. Run gathering sts through center of bra, draw up to desired size and tack securely. Sew bottom edge of bra to top edge of Front. Sew side seams.

Fold I-Cord in half and at cord center, sew to center of bra at top of gathering row. At center back, fold top edge of each section to inside about 3/4" to form cord casing. Sew in place. I-Cord goes from center front over shoulders and then through casing on each side. Tie in a bow.

RED HOT MAMA

*Adapted from a design
by Vashti Braha*

*Just for fun! Make the
three easy pieces and then
decorate them with trims
of fringe and feathers.
What fun to wear!*

RED HOT MAMA

Sizes

One size fits from 28" to 36" bust; garment is stretchy.

Materials

DK or sport weight cotton yarn with elastic component 8 3/4 oz red

Note: *Use of an elasticized yarn is essential for the fit of this garment. Photographed model made with Cascade Yarns Fixation #3629 Red.*

Eyelash yarn with rainbow accents (for trim) 1 3/4 oz red

Note: *Photographed model made with Lion Brand® Fancy Fur #213 Rainbow Red*

1 yard 2" long feather trim (for trim)

Selection of beads of varying sizes and shapes; (for trim)

Jewel-it™ fabric glue (for trim)

Size 22 tapestry needle (to thread beads)

Size G (4mm) crochet hook

Four double point size 10 (6mm) knitting needles

24" Size 10 (6mm) circular knitting needles (or size required for gauge)

Gauge

20 sts = 4" (unstretched) in circular stock st (knit each row)

BLOUSE

INSTRUCTIONS

Starting at bottom, with circular needle CO 140 sts.

EDGING

Rnd 1: Knit; join, making sure work is not twisted. Mark beg of rnd.

Rnd 2: *YO, K2 tog; rep from * around.

Rnd 3: Knit.

Rnd 4: *K2tog, YO; rep from * around.

Rnd 5: Knit.

Rep Rows 2 through 5 until piece measures 2" from CO row.

BODY

Rnd 1: Knit.

Rep Rnd 1, continuing in circular stock st, until piece measures 10" from CO row. BO all sts.

SKIRT

INSTRUCTIONS

With circular needle, starting at bottom, CO 150 sts.

EDGING

Rnd 1: Knit. Join, making sure work is not twisted. Mark beg of rnd.

Rnd 2: *YO, K2 tog; rep from * across.

RED HOT MAMA

Rnd 3: Knit.

Rnd 4: *K2tog, YO; rep from * across.

Rnd 5: Knit.

Rep Rows 2 through 5 until piece measures 2" from CO row.

BODY

Rnd 1: Knit.

Rep Rnd 1, continuing in circular stock st until piece measures 10" from CO row.

EYELET WAIST EDGING

Rnd 1: *K1, *YO, K2tog; rep from * to last st, K1.

Rnds 2 and 3: Purl.

BO all sts.

SLEEVES (make 2)

Starting at bottom, with double point needles CO 40 sts, placing 14 sts on each of 2 needles and 12 sts on 3rd needle. With 4th needle, join sts, making sure work is not twisted. Mark beg of rnd.

EDGING

Rnd 1: Knit.

Rnd 2: *YO, K2 tog; rep from * around.

Rnd 3: Knit.

Rnd 4: *K2tog, YO; rep from * around.

Rnd 5: Knit.

Rep Rnds 2 through 5 until piece measures 1 1/2".

FINISHING

With crochet hook, make a 4-yard chain. Finish off; weave in all ends. Insert chain through eyelets in skirt Eyelet Waist Edging

TRIM

Skirt: Cut yarn used for skirt into random lengths measuring 20" to 24". Following Fringe instructions on page 127, place a strand of yarn in every other space along bottom. Using a tapestry needle, thread beads on some or all of the yarn strands and tie a large enough knot under each bead to secure.

Reserve a 16" piece of feather trim for blouse. Carefully separate feathers from remaining trim. Push a feather up through some of the beads and place a dab of glue at back of feather and glue to knot under bead.

Cut 20" to 24" pieces of eyelash yarn and attach to Skirt edge randomly between fringe.

Blouse: Sew 16" piece of feather trim to upper edge of top. Add fringe, beads and feathers referring to Skirt instructions except cut all yarns 12" to 14".

Sleeves: Add fringe, beads and feathers referring to Skirt instructions except cut yarns 12" to 14".

BODY

Rnd 1: Knit.

Rep Rnd 1, continuing in circular stock st, until piece measures 4" from CO row.

BO all sts.

GLITTER TIME

Designed by Bev Nimon for S. R. Kertzer, Ltd.

Silky and metallic yarns add all the glitter necessary to make this garment glow!

GLITTER TIME

SIZES	Small	Medium	Large
Finished Bust Measurements	36"	40"	44"

Note: *Instructions are written for size Small; changes for sizes Medium and Large are in parentheses.*

Materials:

Metallic Novelty Yarn
   60 (60, 60) g black/silver (Color A)
Silky ribbon yarn
   150 (150, 200) g black (Color B)
Note: *Photographed model made with S. R. Kertzer Baffi #11 Black (A) and S. R. Kertzer Sari #55 Black (B)*
Size 10 (6mm) straight knitting needles
Size 10 1/2 (6.5mm) straight knitting needles (or size required for gauge)
Two size 10 1/2 double-point knitting needles

Gauge

14sts and 20 rows = 4" with larger needles in stock stitch (knit 1 row, purl 1 row) with one strand of each yarn held tog

INSTRUCTIONS

FRONT

Starting at bottom with smaller needles and one strand of each yarn, CO 64 (71, 78) sts. Knit 6 rows.

Change to larger needles and work in stock st for 2" more.

Continue in stock st, dec one st at each end of next row, then every following 5th row 4 times more: 54 (61, 68) sts.

Work even for 2" more; then inc one st at each end of next row, then every following 5th row 4 times: 64 (71, 78) sts.

Work even until piece measures 14 1/2"
(14 1/2", 15") from CO row. Then dec 6
(6, 8) sts evenly spaced across next row.

Change to smaller needles and work 4
rows in K1, P1 rib. BO all sts.

BACK

Work same as front.

FINISHING

Hold back and front with right sides
tog, and sew side seams from bottom
to top.

STRAPS

Following I-Cord instructions on page
126, using both yarns held tog, CO 4
sts and make four cords each 12" long.
Sew two cords to front and and two
cords to back as shown in photo, placing each about 3" in from each side
seam. Tie at shoulders.

SKIRTED BIKINI

Designed by Angela Best

What could be better on a hot summer day than to wear a bikini even if you never jump into the water. And, for a little extra "modesty," complete your bikini with a skirt.

SKIRTED BIKINI

SIZES	Small	Medium	Large
Top A or B cup	32"	34"	36"
Bottom Waist	26"	28"	30"

Note: Instructions are written for size Small; changes for sizes Medium and Large are in parentheses.

Materials

Sport weight cotton yarn
 8 3/4 (8 3/4, 10 1/2) oz orange ombre
Note: Photographed model made with Scheepjes Isis Multi #821
Stitch marker
Size 6 (4mm) straight knitting needles
 (or size required for gauge)
29" Size 10 (6mm) circular knitting needle (for skirt)

Gauge

24 sts = 4" with smaller needles in stock st
 (knit 1 row, purl 1 row)

Stitch Guide

M1 (make 1): Make one st by picking up horizontal bar lying before next st and knitting into back of this lp.

BIKINI TOP

INSTRUCTIONS

FIRST CUP

With smaller needles, CO 20 (26, 30) sts.

Rows 1 through 4: Knit.

Row 5 (wrong side): K3, purl to last 3 sts, K3.

Row 6: Knit.

Rep Rows 5 and 6 until piece measures 2 1/2" (3", 3 1/2") from CO edge, ending by working a knit row.

**Next row: BO 10 (13, 15) sts, continue to work rem sts in patt as established for 2 1/2" (3", 3 1/2") more, then knit 4 rows. BO all sts. **

SECOND CUP

Work as for First Cup until piece measures 2 1/2" (3", 3 1/2"), ending by working a purl row. Then work from ** to ** of First Cup.

FINISHING

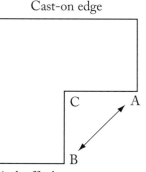

Cast-on edge

C   A

B

Bind-off edge

With right sides facing, join A to B and sew to section C. *Note: The open wedge (A B C section) will be on opposite sides for each cup.*

BORDERS

First Cup:

Row 1: With right side facing and joined wedge at bottom center of work, pick up and knit 20 (26, 30) sts along cast-on edge, M1, place marker, M1, pick up and knit 20 (26, 30) sts along adjacent edge: 42 (54, 62) sts.

Row 2: Purl.

Row 3: K1, YO; work (K2tog, YO) to marker; K1, YO; work (K2tog, YO) to end of row; K1.

Row 4: Purl.

FROM TOP TO BOTTOM

Designed by Margaret Hubert

No need to look drab when the cold winds blow! Dress up from your head to your feet with these bright red accessories that are quick and easy to make.

FROM TOP TO BOTTOM

Sizes

Beret: Fits up to 23" head

Boot Toppers: Adult

Materials

Bulky weight faux fur yarn
   Beret: 3 1/2 oz red
   Boot Toppers: 5 1/4 oz red
Worsted weight yarn
   Beret: 3 oz red
   Boot Toppers: 3 oz red
Note: *Photographed model
   made with Lion Brand®
   Fun Fur #113 Red and
   Lion Brand® Wool-Ease®
   #102 Ranch Red*
Size 8 (5mm) knitting
   needles (or size required
   for gauge)
Size 10 1/2 (6.5mm)
   knitting needles

Gauge

14 sts in K1, P1 ribbing
   (unstretched) = 3" with
   smaller needles and
   worsted weight yarn

BERET

INSTRUCTIONS

Starting at bottom of cuff with smaller needles and worsted weight yarn, CO 84 sts.

Work in K1, P1 ribbing for 4". Change to fur yarn and larger needles.

Increase Row: Knit, inc 10 sts evenly spaced across: 94 sts.

Work even in garter st (knit every row) until piece measures 9" from cast-on row.

SHAPE CROWN

Row 1: Dec 4 sts evenly spaced: 90 sts.

Row 2: *K13, K2 tog; rep from * across: 84 sts.

Rows 3, 5, 7, 9, and 11: Knit even.

Row 4: *K12 , K2tog; rep from * across: 78 sts.

Row 6: *K11, K2tog; rep from * across: 72 sts.

Row 8: *K10, K2tog; rep from * across: 66 sts.

Row 10: *K9, K2tog; rep from * across: 60 sts.

Row 12: *K8, K2tog, rep from * across: 54 sts.

Row 13: * K2tog; rep from * across: 27 sts.

Row 14: K1, *K2tog; rep from * across: 14 sts.

Cut yarn, leaving an 18" end for sewing. Thread yarn into a tapestry needle and draw yarn through rem sts on needle; draw up tightly and secure; sew seam to cuff.

With worsted weight yarn, sew cuff seam; turn cuff 2" to inside and stitch down all around.

BOOT TOPPERS

INSTRUCTIONS (make 2)

Starting at bottom of cuff with worsted weight yarn and smaller needles, CO 48 sts.

Work in K1, P1 ribbing for 2 inches.

Change to larger needles and fur yarn.

Knit one row, inc one st at each side. Work in garter st (knit every row), inc one st each side every 2" three times more: 56 sts. Work even in garter st until piece measures 12" from cast-on row.

Change to smaller needles and worsted weight yarn. Work in K1, P1 ribbing for 3". BO loosely in ribbing. Mark this end for top cuff.

FINISHING

Sew back seam. To wear, turn bottom cuff to inside, slip over boots; tuck top cuff to inside of boot.

CABLED TUBE TOP

Designed by Joan Somerville for Cascade Yarns

The cables and the elastic yarn give this tube top its shape.

CABLED TUBE TOP

Sizes

One size fits from 28" to 36" bust;
garment is stretchy.

Materials

DK or sport weight cotton yarn with
elastic component
3 1/2 oz pink
*Note: Use of an elasticized yarn is essential for
the fit of this garment.*
Photographed model made with Cascade
Yarns Fixation #3077 Pink
Stitch marker
Cable needle
24" Size 6 (4 mm) circular knitting needle
(or size required for gauge)

Gauge

24 sts = 4" in pattern

Stitch Guide

Increase: Knit in front and back of st:
Inc made.

Cable 4 Front (C4F): Sl next 2 sts to cable
needle and hold in front of work; K2, then
K2 from cable needle: C4F made.

Cable 4 Front Increase (C4FI): Sl next 2
sts to cable needle and hold in front of
work; inc in each of next 2 knit stitches on
needle; then inc in each knit stitch from
cable needle: 8 sts: C4FI made.

INSTRUCTIONS

Starting at bottom, CO 160 sts; join, being
careful not to twist sts. Mark beg of rnds.

FOUNDATION

Rnd 1: Knit.

Rnd 2: *P2, K4, P2; rep from * around.

BODY

Rnd 1 (cable rnd): *P2, C4F, P2; rep from * around.

Rnds 2, 3 and 4: *P2, K4, P2; rep from * around.

Rep Body Rnds 1 through 4 until piece measures 3 3/4", ending by working Rnd 4 of pattern.

Increase Rnd 1: P2, CF4, P2; *P2, C4FI, P2, (P2, C4F, P2) 3 times; rep from * around, ending last rep with P2, C4FI, P2, (P2, C4F, P2) twice: 180 sts.

Increase Rnd 2: P2, K4, P2 *P2, (inc) twice, P4, (inc) twice, P2, (P2, K4, P2) 3 times; rep from * around, ending last rep with P2, (inc) twice, P4 (inc) twice, P2, (P2, K4, P2) twice: 200 sts.

Continue in patt as established until piece measures 8 1/2", ending by working a Row 2 of cable patt.

TOP SHAPING

Rnd 1: P2, K4, P2, *P2 (K2tog) twice, P4, (K2tog) twice, P2, (P2, K4, P2) 3 times; rep from *, ending last rep with (P2, K4, P2) 2 times: 180 sts.

Rnd 2: P2, K4, P2, *P2, (K2tog) 4times, P2, (P2, K4, P2) 3 times; rep from *, ending last rep with P2, K4, P2) 2 times: 160 sts.

Rnd 3 (cable rnd): *P2, C4F, P2; rep from * around.

Rnd 4: *P2, K4, P2; rep from * around. BO all sts.

EMPRESS HALTER

Designed by Rebecca Hatcher

Whether it's working in the garden or dancing on the town, you'll look like royalty when you wear this easy-to-make halter top.

EMPRESS HALTER

SIZES	Small	Medium	Large
Body Bust Measurements	30"- 32"	34"- 36"	38"- 40"
Finished Bust Measurements	31"	35"	39"

Note: Instructions are written for size Small; changes for sizes Medium and Large are in parentheses.

Note: Garment is stretchy.

Materials

Worsted weight mercerized cotton
  400 (500, 600) yds multicolor
Note: Photographed model made with Schaefer Yarn Company Laurel Empress Wu Zhao.
2 stitch markers
36" Size 8 (5mm) circular knitting needle
  (or size required for gauge)
36" Size 7 (4.5mm) circular knitting needle
  (or one size smaller than size required for gauge)

Gauge

19 sts = 4" with larger needles in circular stock st
  (knit all rows)

INSTRUCTIONS

BOTTOM BORDERS

First Border: With larger needle, CO 84 (94, 104) sts.

Knit 7 rows. Cut yarn, and transfer sts temporarily to smaller needle.

Second Border: With larger needle, CO 84 (94, 104) sts. Knit 8 rows, place marker on needle, then knit across sts of First Border: 168 (188, 208) sts now on the larger needle. Place another marker to indicate beg of rnd, join.

BODY

Knit 13 rnds even.

Decrease Rnd: * K1, SSK, knit to 3 sts before next marker, K2tog, K1, sl marker; rep from * once: 164 (184, 204) sts.

Rep last 14 rnds 3 times more: 152 (172, 192) sts.

Knit even until piece measures 9 1/2" (10 1/2", 11 1/2") from CO edge.

Shape Bodice

Knit to 10 sts before first marker. Place 66 (76, 86) sts just worked on scrap yarn temporarily for Back.

Bodice is now worked flat in rows on rem 86 (96, 106) sts.

Decrease Row: K1, K2tog, knit even across: 85 (95, 105) sts.

Rep Decrease Row 45 (55, 65) times more; BO rem 40 sts.

Top Edge Trim

With smaller needles, CO 80 sts for right strap, pick up 30 (35, 40) sts down right side of bodice, K66 (76, 86) sts for Back from scrap yarn, pick up 30 (35, 40) sts up left side of bodice, CO 80 sts for left strap: 286 (306, 326) sts. Knit 4 rows even. BO.

I'VE GOT A SECRET NIGHTIE

Designed by Dawn Adcock

Don't tell – but a lace heart hides behind the inset panel on this simple, snuggly-soft nightie! The garment is easy to adjust for many sizes with the straps along the back.

I'VE GOT A SECRET NIGHTIE

SIZES	Small	Medium	Large	X-Large	XX-Large
Finished Bust Measurements	32"	40"	48"	56"	64"

Note: Instructions are written for size Small; changes for sizes Medium, Large, X-Large, and XX-Large are in parentheses.

Note: Size is adjustable by use of ties that connect in back and take in extra ease in width.

Materials

Worsted weight yarn
   12 (12, 18, 18, 18) oz raspberry
*Note: Photographed model made with TLC® Amoré™
   #3908 Raspberry*
2 Stitch markers
2 Safety pins
Size J (6 mm) crochet hook
36" Size 10½ (6.5 mm) circular knitting needle
   (or size required for gauge)

Gauge

12 sts and 16 rows = 4" in stock st
   (knit 1 row, purl 1 row)

Stitch Guide

SSK (slip, slip, knit): Slip 2 sts as to knit one at a time to right-hand needle. Insert tip of left-hand needle into fronts of these 2 sts and knit them tog: SSK decrease made.

INSTRUCTIONS

RUFFLED BORDER

Note: Use a loose and stretchy cast on to allow the ruffle to scallop fully. For photographed model, edge of cast on was gently stretched out after the ruffle was completed.

Starting at bottom, CO 192 (240, 288, 336, 384) sts loosely; do not join, work back and forth in rows.

Row 1: Knit.

Row 2 (right side): Knit.

Row 3: Purl.

I'VE GOT A SECRET NIGHTIE

Row 4: *K2tog; rep from * across: 96 (120, 144, 168, 192) sts.

BODY

Row 1: K4, purl to last 4 sts, K4.

Row 2 (right side): Knit.

Rep Rows 1 and 2 of until piece measures 20" (or 1" less than total length desired).

EYELET EDGE

Rows 1 through 3: Knit.

Row 4 (right side): K1; *K2tog, YO, K2; rep from * to last 3 sts, YO, K2tog, K1.

Rows 5 and 6: Knit.

BO loosely.

HEART INSET PANEL

Ruffled Border

CO 60 (66, 72, 78, 84) sts loosely.

Row 1: Knit.

Row 2 (right side): Knit. Mark this row as right side.

Row 3: Purl.

Row 4: *K2tog; rep from * across: 30 (33, 36, 39, 42) sts.

Body

Knit all rows for garter stitch panel until piece measures 16" (or 5" less than total length of Body), ending by working a wrong-side row.

Begin Heart Panel: K10 (11, 13, 14, 16), place marker; work Row 1 of heart chart, place marker, K9 (11, 12, 14, 15).

Work 11 more rows of heart panel chart by knitting to marker, work chart over sts to next marker, knit to end. After completing chart, knit until piece measures 20" from beginning, (or 1" less than length of main body piece), ending by working a right-side row. BO as to knit.

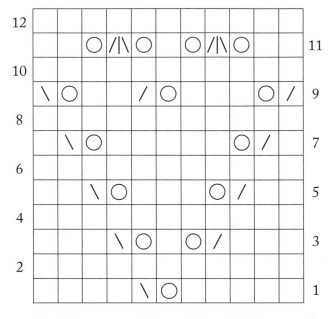

Blank Square = Knit on RS and WS

○ = Yarn Over

／ = K2tog

＼ = SSK

／|＼ = Sl 2tog k-wise, k1, p2sso

FINISHING

Lay out main Body with side edges folded to center front. Place inset heart panel under the front folded panels, centered in the front body. Pin inset panel to main body at top corner edges of inset panel; these corners are about where bra straps would normally be positioned. Front outer flaps of main body should each measure 5", (5 1/2", 6", 6 1/2", 7") from top edge center corner to edge where pinned to panel underneath. Sew each corner of inset panel in place along top edge for 1", connecting the panel to the outer body wrap on each front side.

SHOULDER TIES

With right side facing, pick up and knit 4 sts on sewn corner along top edge.

Rows 1 and 2: Knit.

Row 3: K1, K2tog, K1: 3 sts.

Row 4: Knit.

Row 5: K1, K2tog: 2 sts.

Row 6: Knit.

Row 7: K2tog.

Place rem st on crochet hook and ch for 36". Finish off; weave in ends.

Work a 2nd tie on opposite body side corner in same manner.

Center Front Ties: With crochet hook, join yarn at top corner edge of main body panel. Ch for 20". Finish off; weave in ends. Repeat for other center front tie.

To wear: Bring shoulder ties up and over shoulder, then straight down back to the first corresponding eyelet hole. Insert tie through this hole and then weave in and out of next holes towards the center, ending at center back. Rep for opposite side. Tie these together at center back, adjusting the width by taking in any ease for a custom fit. Tie front center ties over inset heart panel to close front.

A LITTLE NIGHT MUSIC

Designed by Margaret Hubert

Perfect for dancing, dining or dating, this little dress will take you on memorable evenings and romantic adventures.

A LITTLE NIGHT MUSIC

SIZES	Small	Medium	Large
Body Bust Measurements	30"- 32"	32"- 34"	34"- 36"
Finished Bust Measurements	33"	34"	35"

Note: *Instructions are written for size Small; changes for sizes Medium and Large are in parentheses.*

Materials

DK or sport weight yarn
  19 1/4 (19 1/4, 21) oz black
Note: *Photographed model made with Patons® Grace #60040 Night*
Size 6 (4mm) knitting needles (or size
  required for gauge)
Size 8 (5mm) knitting needles

Gauge

6 sts = 1" with smaller needles in stock st (knit 1 row,
  purl 1 row)

INSTRUCTIONS

BACK

With smaller needles, starting at hemline, CO 114 (120, 126) sts.

Work in stock st until piece measures 15 1/2" (16", 16 1/2"), ending by working a purl row.

Next row: Dec 1 st each side, and rep the dec every 4th row 9 (10, 11) times more: 94 (98, 102) sts.

Work even until piece measures 23 1/2" (24", 24 1/2"). Then inc one st each side and rep the inc every other row, 2 (3, 4) times more: 100 (106, 112) sts.

Work even until piece measures 25" (26", 27"); ending by working a purl row.

ARMHOLES

Row 1: BO 8 (10, 12) sts, work across row: 92 (96, 100) sts.

Row 2: Rep Row 1: 84 (86, 88) sts.

Row 3: K1, sl 1, K1, PSSO, knit to last 3 sts, K2 tog, K1.

Row 4: Purl.

Rep Row 3 and 4 until 40 (42, 44) sts rem. BO.

FRONT

Work same as Back through Row 4 of Armholes: 82 (84, 86) sts.

DIVIDE FOR NECK

Dividing Row: K1, sl 1, K1, PSSO; K36 (37, 38), K2 tog; join a new ball of yarn, K2tog, K36 (37, 38), K2tog, K1. There are now 40 (41, 42) sts on each side of front. Working each side with a separate ball of yarn, dec at armhole edges same as back and AT THE SAME TIME, K2tog at each neck edge, every other row, until 4 sts rem on each side; K2tog twice. BO.

NECK RUFFLE

First Layer

With larger needles, CO 90 sts; change to smaller needles.

Row 1: Knit, inc in every st: 180 sts.

Row 2: Purl.

Rows 3 and 4: Rep Rows 1 and 2: 360 sts.

Row 5: Knit, inc in every other st: 540 sts.

Row 6: Purl.

Row 7: *K1, YO, K2 tog; rep from * across row.

Row 8: Purl.

Row 9: Knit.

Rows 10 through 13: Rep Rows 6 through 9.

Row 14: Purl.

BO with larger needles.

Second Layer

Work same as first layer, except rep Rows 13 and 14 once more. BO with larger needles.

TIES (make 2)

With larger needles, CO 6 sts. Work in stock st for 12". BO. Ties will twist inward, forming an open tube.

FINISHING

Sew side seams from bottom to top, reversing the first inch of seam at bottom. Roll of the stockinette st forms hemline.

Place First Layer of ruffle piece on top of 2nd layer, with right sides up. Sew tog at CO edges to form double ruffle.

Pin straight edge of ruffle to tip of Left Front; leave a 1" space for shoulder, pin ruffle along back neck edge, leave a one inch space for right shoulder, pin ruffle along right front to center of V. Leaving left neck plain, fold rem length of ruffle back up to center of "V" and tack in place. Sew ruffle securely to neckline.

Sew ties to left shoulder, at end of ruffle, tie in a knot.

BODACIOUS BUSTIER

Adapted by Rita Weiss from a design by Marnie MacLean

*Very easy-to-make
and very easy-to-wear,
a great addition to any
girl's wardrobe.*

GENERAL DIRECTIONS

Terms

Finish off—This means to end your piece by pulling the yarn through the last loop remaining on the needle. This will prevent the work from unraveling.

Continue in Pattern as Established—This means to follow the pattern stitch as if has been set up, working any increases or decreases in such a way that the pattern remains the same as it was established.

Work even—This means that the work is continued in the pattern as established without increasing or decreasing.

Right Side—This means the side of the garment that will be seen.

Wrong Side—This means the side of the garment that is inside when the garment is worn.

Right Front—This means the part of the garment that will be worn on the right side of the body.

Left Front—This means the part of the garment that will be worn on the left side of the body.

The patterns in this book have been written using the knitting terminology that is used in the United States. Terms which may have different equivalents in other parts of the world are listed below.

United States	International
Gauge	tension
Skip	miss
Yarn over (YO)	yarn forward (yfwd)
Bind off	Cast off

Gauge

This is probably the most important aspect of knitting!

GAUGE simply means the number of stitches per inch, and the numbers of rows per inch that result from a specified yarn worked with needles in a specified size. But since everyone knits —some loosely, some tightly, some in-between—the measurements of individual work can vary greatly, even when the knitters use the same pattern and the same size yarn and or needle.

If you don't work to the gauge specified in the pattern, your project will never be the correct size, and you may not have enough yarn to finish your project. Needle sizes given in instructions are merely guides, and should never be used without a gauge swatch.

To make a gauge swatch, knit a swatch that is about 4" square, using the suggested needle and the number of stitches given in the pattern. Measure your swatch. If the number of stitches is fewer than those listed in the pattern, try making another swatch with a smaller needle. If the number of stitches is more than is called for in the pattern, try making another swatch with a larger needle. It is your responsibility to make sure you achieve the gauge specified in the pattern.

I-Cord

Cord is worked from the right side only; do not turn. Stitches will fold toward the wrong side to form a double thickness cord.

CO 3 sts on one double-point knitting needle.

Row 1: With another double-point, K3; do not turn. Slide sts to opposite end of the needle.

Row 2: Take yarn around the back side of sts and with 2nd needle, K3; do not turn. Slide sts to opposite end of needle.

Rep Rows 1 and 2 until the cord is the desired length. BO.

Knitting Needles Conversion Chart

U.S.	0	1	2	3	4	5	6	7	8	9	10	10½	11	13	15	17
Metric	2	2.25	2.75	3.25	3.5	3.75	4	4.5	5	5.5	6	6.5	8	9	10	12.75